the journey is the reward.

—TAOIST SAYING

recorded by:

bag•gage (bag´ij), *n.*, **1.** the trunks, bags, parcels, and suitcases in which one carries one's belongings while traveling; luggage. **2.** superfluous or burdensome practices, regulations, ideas, or traits.

dates:

destination:

accommodations:

traveling companions:

highlights:

dates:

destination:

accommodations:

traveling companions:

highlights:

dates:

destination:

accommodations:

traveling companions:

highlights:

dates:

destination:

accommodations:

traveling companions:

highlights:

dates:

destination:

accommodations:

traveling companions:

highlights:

—dates:

—destination:

—accommodations:

—traveling companions:

—highlights:

we are all travelers in the wilderness of this world, and the best we can find in our travels is an honest friend.

—ROBERT LOUIS STEVENSON

where i want to go: tuscany * des moines *

istanbul * moscow * coney island * paris * london * sheboygan

what exotic locales are you dreaming of?

ex•plore (ik-splôr´, -splor´), *v.*

ex•plored, ex•plor•ing,

ex•plores 1. to seek for or

after; to strive to attain by

search; to look wisely and

carefully for. **2.** to search

through or into; to penetrate

or range over for discovery.

— dates:

— destination:

— accommodations:

— traveling companions:

— highlights:

dates:

destination:

accommodations:

traveling companions:

highlights:

dates:

destination:

accommodations:

traveling companions:

highlights:

dates:

destination:

accommodations:

traveling companions:

highlights:

dates:

destination:

accommodations:

traveling companions:

highlights:

dates:

destination:

accommodations:

traveling companions:

highlights:

the worst thing about being a
tourist is having other tourists
recognize you as a tourist.

—RUSSELL BAKER

sched•ule (skej´ o͞ol) *n.,* **1**. a list of times of departures and arrivals; a timetable. **2**. a plan for performing work or achieving an objective, specifying the order and allotted time for each part.

— dates:

— destination:

— accommodations:

— traveling companions:

— highlights:

dates:

destination:

accommodations:

traveling companions:

highlights:

dates:

destination:

accommodations:

traveling companions:

highlights:

dates:

destination:

accommodations:

traveling companions:

highlights:

dates:

destination:

accommodations:

traveling companions:

highlights:

dates:

destination:

accommodations:

traveling companions:

highlights:

though we travel the world over to find the beautiful, we must carry it with us, or we find it not.

—RALPH WALDO EMERSON

all the places i've been: * whether it's your first time out of town or your fifth visit to Europe, every destination is worth remembering.

tip (tip), *n.*, *v.* **tipped**, **tip•ping**, **tips 1.** a small sum of money given to someone for performing a service; a gratuity. **2.** a piece of confidential, advance, or inside information. **3.** a helpful hint.

— dates:

— destination:

— accommodations:

— traveling companions:

— highlights:

dates:

destination:

accommodations:

traveling companions:

highlights:

dates:

destination:

accommodations:

traveling companions:

highlights:

dates:

destination:

accommodations:

traveling companions:

highlights:

dates: _____

destination: _____

accommodations: _____

traveling companions: _____

highlights: _____

dates:

destination:

accommodations:

traveling companions:

highlights:

the whole object of travel is not to
set foot on foreign land; it is at last
to set foot on one's own country as a
foreign land.

—G.K. CHESTERTON

re•new (ri nōo´, -nyōo´) *v.*

re•newed, re•new•ing, re•news

1. to make new or as if new again; restore. **2.** to regain or restore the physical or mental vigor of; revive. **3.** to bring into being again; reestablish.

— dates:

— destination:

— accommodations:

— traveling companions:

— highlights:

dates:

destination:

accommodations:

traveling companions:

highlights:

dates:

destination:

accommodations:

traveling companions:

highlights:

dates:

destination:

accommodations:

traveling companions:

highlights:

dates:

destination:

accommodations:

traveling companions:

highlights:

dates:

destination:

accommodations:

traveling companions:

highlights:

even the elephant carries but a small trunk on his journeys. the perfection of traveling is to travel without baggage.

—HENRY DAVID THOREAU

where i ate: * it's a fact: food tastes better on vacation. savor every bite and remember to remember it. *

i•tin•er•ar•y (i tin´ əṛer´ē)

n., **1.** a route or proposed route of a journey. **2.** an account or record of a journey. **3.** a guidebook for travelers.

— dates:

— destination:

— accommodations:

— traveling companions:

— highlights:

dates:

destination:

accommodations:

traveling companions:

highlights:

dates:

destination:

accommodations:

traveling companions:

highlights:

dates:

destination:

accommodations:

traveling companions:

highlights:

—dates: ——————————————

—destination: ——————————————

—accommodations: ——————————————

—traveling companions: ——————————————

—highlights: ——————————————

dates:

destination:

accommodations:

traveling companions:

highlights:

a journey is like marriage. the
certain way to be wrong is to
think you control it.

—JOHN STEINBECK

en•joy (en joi') *v.* **1.** to receive pleasure or satisfaction from. **2.** to have the use or benefit of: *enjoys good health. Int. v.* **1.** to have a pleasurable or satisfactory time.

dates:

destination:

accommodations:

traveling companions:

highlights:

dates:

destination:

accommodations:

traveling companions:

highlights:

dates: _____

destination: _____

accommodations: _____

traveling companions: _____

highlights: _____

dates:

destination:

accommodations:

traveling companions:

highlights:

dates:

destination:

accommodations:

traveling companions:

highlights:

dates:

destination:

accommodations:

traveling companions:

highlights:

i have found out that there ain't no
surer way to find out whether you
like people or hate them than to
travel with them.

—MARK TWAIN

where I shopped/what I bought:

*tip: pack an empty bag in your luggage . . . this could be the shopping trip of a lifetime. *

cus•toms (kus´təms) *n.,* **1.**
practices followed by people
of a particular group or
region. **2.** duties or taxes
imposed on imported and,
less commonly, exported
goods.

— dates:

— destination:

— accommodations:

— traveling companions:

— highlights:

dates:

destination:

accommodations:

traveling companions:

highlights:

dates:

destination:

accommodations:

traveling companions:

highlights:

dates:

destination:

accommodations:

traveling companions:

highlights:

dates:

destination:

accommodations:

traveling companions:

highlights:

dates:

destination:

accommodations:

traveling companions:

highlights:

all of life is a foreign country.

—JACK KEROUAC

sou•ve•nir (sōō´və nēr´, sōō´ və nēr´), *n.* **1.** that which serves as a reminder; a remembrancer; a memento; a keep sake. **2.** something of sentimental value. **3.** a reminder of past events.

— dates:

— destination:

— accommodations:

— traveling companions:

— highlights:

dates:

destination:

accommodations:

traveling companions:

highlights:

dates:

destination:

accommodations:

traveling companions:

highlights:

dates: _____

destination: _____

accommodations: _____

traveling companions: _____

highlights: _____

dates:

destination:

accommodations:

traveling companions:

highlights:

dates:

destination:

accommodations:

traveling companions:

highlights:

it is better to travel hopefully
than arrive.

—ROBERT LOUIS STEVENSON

best travel books/websites:

* trust the experts. a little planning will go a long way. *

first class (fûrst´ klăs´) *n.,*

1. the most luxurious and most expensive class of accommodations on a train, passenger ship, airplane, or other conveyance.

— dates:

— destination:

— accommodations:

— traveling companions:

— highlights:

dates:

destination:

accommodations:

traveling companions:

highlights:

dates: _____

destination: _____

accommodations: _____

traveling companions: _____

highlights: _____

dates:

destination:

accommodations:

traveling companions:

highlights:

dates: _____

destination: _____

accommodations: _____

traveling companions: _____

highlights: _____

dates:

destination:

accommodations:

traveling companions:

highlights:

my favorite thing is to go
where I've never been.
—DIANE ARBUS

ex•pe•ri•ence (ik spēr´ē əns)

n., **1.** active participation in events or activities, leading to the accumulation of knowledge or skill. **2.** An event or a series of events participated in or lived through.

dates:

destination:

accommodations:

traveling companions:

highlights:

dates:

destination:

accommodations:

traveling companions:

highlights:

— dates:

— destination:

— accommodations:

— traveling companions:

— highlights:

dates:

destination:

accommodations:

traveling companions:

highlights:

—dates: —————————————————

—destination: —————————————

—accommodations: —————————

—traveling companions: ————

—highlights: ————————————

dates:

destination:

accommodations:

traveling companions:

highlights:

travel is fatal to prejudice, bigotry,
and narrow-mindedness.

—MARK TWAIN

top ten favorite hotels: * marble baths and ocean views don't always a great hotel make. where are some of your favorites? *

con•cierge (kon´sē ērzh´) *n.*, a staff member of a hotel or apartment complex who assists guests or residents, as by handling the storage of luggage, taking and delivering messages, and making reservations.

— dates:

— destination:

— accommodations:

— traveling companions:

— highlights:

dates:

destination:

accommodations:

traveling companions:

highlights:

dates:

destination:

accommodations:

traveling companions:

highlights:

dates:

destination:

accommodations:

traveling companions:

highlights:

dates:

destination:

accommodations:

traveling companions:

highlights:

—dates:

—destination:

—accommodations:

—traveling companions:

—highlights:

i have been a stranger
in a strange land.

—MOSES, EXODUS 2:22

mem•o•ry (mem´ə rē) **1.** the mental faculty of retaining and recalling past experience. **2.** the act or an instance of remembering; recollections.

— dates:

— destination:

— accommodations:

— traveling companions:

— highlights:

dates:

destination:

accommodations:

traveling companions:

highlights:

dates:

destination:

accommodations:

traveling companions:

highlights:

dates:

destination:

accommodations:

traveling companions:

highlights:

dates:

destination:

accommodations:

traveling companions:

highlights:

—dates: —————————————————————————————

—destination: ———————————————————————

— accommodations: ——————————————————

—traveling companions: ——————————————

—highlights: —————————————————————————

if we are always arriving and
departing, it is also true that we are
eternally anchored. one's destination is never a place but rather a
new way of looking at things.

—HENRY MILLER

top ten roadside attractions: * It's amazing how the definition of "attraction" varies from place to place. Record all those amazing sights you've seen. *

tour•ist trap (tŏŏr´ist trăp) *n.*, a place, such as a shop or resort area, that offers over-priced goods and services to tourists.

— dates: _____

— destination: _____

— accommodations: _____

— traveling companions: _____

— highlights: _____

dates:

destination:

accommodations:

traveling companions:

highlights:

dates:

destination:

accommodations:

traveling companions:

highlights:

dates:

destination:

accommodations:

traveling companions:

highlights:

dates:

destination:

accommodations:

traveling companions:

highlights:

dates:

destination:

accommodations:

traveling companions:

my thoughts:

books

Barry, Dave. DAVE BARRY'S ONLY TRAVEL GUIDE YOU'LL EVER NEED. New York: Ballantine Books, 1999.

De Botton, Alain. THE ART OF TRAVEL. New York: Vintage, 2004.

Famie, Keith. YOU REALLY HAVEN'T BEEN THERE UNTIL YOU'VE EATEN THE FOOD . New York: Clarkson Potter, 2003.

Fodors. FODORS' 1,0001 SMART TRAVEL TIPS. New York: Fodors, 2003.

Blanchard, Melinda and Robert. A TRIP TO THE BEACH. New York: Three Rivers Press, 2001.

websites

http://www.fodors.com

http://www.lonelyplanet.com

http://www.travel.state.gov/

time to pack your bags

designed by jan derevjanik

written by kerri buckley

www.clarksonpotter.com

isbn: 1-4000-8173-4

potter style